This book is dedicated to the memory of Susan Kallenborn.

Acknowledgements

Some of these poems have appeared in or have been accepted by *Bloomsbury Review, Cha-Cha Review, Cream City Review, The Plough: North Coast Review, Soundings, Wellspring* and in the anthology, *Wrestling with the Angel* (Baker, Gwynn, eds.).

Table of Contents

Preface

The challenge is to live in the presence of Christ in Cleveland while plastering, roofing, driving a cab, sitting in the corner bar. It is to maintain an eternal perspective wrapped in the fulness of the temporal. This is an ordinary enough challenge in the Christian faith —to know the indwelling of Christ in all, and to sense with awe the power which sustains all things. Ordinary though it is, the challenge is seldom well met, for the rush of the senses generate the illusions all religions must deal with.

David Craig is a psalmist who praises the complexity of the way, as St. John of the Cross once celebrated its darkness, as Gerald Manley Hopkins celebrated the strangeness and depth of the visions which burst one through illusion, and into the grace of understanding. Craig is wholly of this century; he knows all stand outside time, and locked in flesh, and knows this glory and its transience. He sees the surfaces of the world, and knows the substance which underlies these surfaces. I believe David Craig to be the foremost religious poet of the day whose special gift is to reveal the presence and care of God in all things — especially the most unlikely things. He gives us poems as rich in humanity as they are of the mystery of God, which is the same. He is doing the work he was called for, and we are blessed by the presence his words generate.

Howard McCord

1

SUN

New York in Broad Daylight
(for Jack)

In sunny Central Park
I see Him,
a Child flying a Japanese kite,
the kite itself. Pot-bellied,
He plays a hot corner.

He waves beneath His chin,
jogs uphill with the horde and I feel
all the grass growing inside me.
Great grey buildings
become mice. Blind, they crawl, new-born,
squeaking. Paintings along the sidewalk
learn French, drink coffee.

A Julliard student plays viola
to my violin:
the careful crunch of cheesecake,
Village cafe. And later,
all the small people inside me bop,
the Flintstone theme on sax, Washington Park.
I see Him, with brush and can,
face streaked,
as billowing orange letters,
noisy cars, zip past.

Young Monk (Denver)

Wine, water,
like the red patch, yellow body of a peach
in a bowl, sit
behind layers of fine lacquer,
two millenia of pews
in the bowels of the dark Catholic
Church.
And on the cross up front,
on the wall behind the gold,
the altar, I feel the body, the wound,
in new water, draw;
feel the corresponding motion
without noise.

Mass and, after, outside,
capped clothespins hold the flapping
bedsheet canvass, day: yellow sun head
tucked in a coat of trailing,
above-the-trees, wrap-around blue.
Garrulous birds and the sweet
smell of pine needle.

A calling. Fine as my stride,
elevated as the caps of waves,
spray and shingle, celibate air.

This life for Life
and a walk through the trees.

...the praise which is

a thousand mosquitoes, their silver droppings
to the river, the ripples;
is assembly lines on the banks under trees,
the clanking, seeds twirling down;
small dimes shining in the mud, or the
faces of thin, French nuns in procession,
fortune tellers with the Infant of Prague
in store front windows;
it is the clear apprehension
of a rotten, flagging fencepost, and the strung wire
which binds the sky on measured knots, small wrists.

Wrens gambol in the woodbine,
in the mouthings of syllables which, just now,
it seemed, we had spoken as if with our own mouths;
are honey, down through the tall trees,
lolling on the flowers, or Roman
boots marching through Gaul, a beachball
in the sand.

All this in a child
watching his hand, moving.

Where the Houses Lean to Greet You

The uncombed blond rage of the little girl
next door finds the enemy it needs
in dirty hands, face. Her threadbare clothes
upset her. And yesterday, I saw her stand
despite herself, against three kids, with rocks.
Her brother had to pull her away.
She has a big-eared puppy named Chuckster,
who cries as she jerks his chain,
tries to coax him down concrete steps.

This morning, though, she smiled back,
and like bread, rose, brightly met, through dirt,
the her she knows, waits for.

speaking dog

A man follows. His Dane lopes,
all tongue, up to the other side
of the fence he
pretends to be smelling.
I know better, and
how to play:
slide glances,
sniff and fade.

taxi 2

A silver silo, beneath snowy
scythes: a mountain peak,
farmhouse roof; behind
a blustering rib of trees,
pulses, a red heart
in the snow.

Later, geese pierce
a crab-blue sky. Great white
mountains sound above the still
iced rims, the water craters along
shaded curbs in these
axle-pounding streets.

Parked Taxi
(6:30 am)

A skiff of wind: the side of a ship
skidding into port and long dead leaves
over curbs: the tide.

"Board's clear."
I watch a dark argument going on
in the tops of these trees, a determined tossing;
and on the FM, as if to answer, violins and orchestra!

I wait,
want to play this oaten flute for the crows
in that field,
for the grey and seedless days
which number twenty five in my opened palm.

I curl in the Checker seat,
a pad on my lap, and like Li Po,
toss in the stems of these
mountain flowers.

33rd Birthday Poem
(for Don Miller)

1)
Even
on a sailboat blue, Colorado winter
afternoon, wind and the flap in pantleg.
Great curling petals: the sky.
And off the highway, cold
water.
Muskrat diving, sensing me
above tall straw grass,
roadside concrete duct.

2)
Tree bark: a mass of sinew:
the power in creation.

Driving taxi,
other trees, distant,
like small irregular stones against the pre-dawn,
high plains sky;
toward the center of that horizon,
the slow gathering of orange from
the russet, the pinks.

Steering wheel, the backs of my hands...

11

3)
My 33rd
and tonight, one of my fares
walked up to a guy on his doorstep,
decked him. He then turned crisply,
walked back to the cab.

Something about (the politics of) five grand.

The ignorance I feel wrapped in
is dark. It's like
a call to dance in the twilight,
waiting for stars, the faint
stirrings of mushrooms.

Sealed Days

Crisp brown leaves, crabs scratching along
the pavement.
Tomes wrested from pitched iron:
bars of grey sky.
Hills, bowed, strung, crowned in rock, teeth.

You heal.
Strength out of cold night air,
the pure sear in grating wheels.

*

The mountain rises in shoots of shale.
Wedged fields rise, turn,
each grinds on its axis;

morning comes,
carried as it is, in the mouths of birds.

*

At the foot of tourniquet hills
the scrubbed brush ascends through red ash,
pails of yellow grass.
Distant mountains nod,
brute chorus in the finite sun.
This work, this 99 degrees,

13

dry as hollowed bones where
we haul up chunks of basement concrete
in five gallon buckets,
over shaft of window well,
bruised window frame,
run them, two at a time
to the street.

At the lawn hose
below magnetic hills, Living Water springs up
from a tomb of cool purple cells,
fountains over rock and rib
easing parchment earth.

*

At week's end, the autumn sun still hot,

a cold one on the table.
I lie on the cool floor, next to the aquarium,
plaster still on my clothes, hands.
The sky is ornate blue,
a breeze washes in.

Tears are the gifts a lover brings.

*

I will wait for You.
The past will drop in jewels from my hands,
the past will drop.

And all these misshapen stones, tangled
jade green kelp will recede,
sea rings and fingers,
past this thin wet necklace, will
revolve in the belly of that blue tourquoise,
beached whale.

Come, like new.
Your laughter over the water,
Your gaze above the burning sea.

*

Boards and hooks heave and groan.

From this porch swing,
the sun, gone,
leaves its pink to walk the dark and settled roofs;

purple moves to the west as
pale stars
torch the loose strings of sealed days.

*

15

Here is peace, in darkness,
where the passage of time is as falling leaves.

Here is the fizz in dark foam, duned prints;
here, the gnarl in driftwood,
a white bird on a dark shore.

Cleveland

Rises:
the Sohio, National City, Huntington Bank:
shoulders nudging, great white galleys in
an ocean mined red in cuts and coral,
hot copper solder, long digital mornings.

In traffic, the number 6 bus,
sewer caps, the warm orange of the engines;
down 9th: river whistles, temperature readings,
a house in every passing eye, the kraut and dogs,
the commerce of bread and utensils, minus any sway
toward the slow moving rains.

On sunny days, there is a keyboard
in the independent movement
of flowers, in the bright yellow and black jacket:
vibrations, the colors of bees;
old Gaelic crosses, courtyards.
            Listen...
on a quiet evening, you can hear it
in the knocking of moored boats all
the way to Sandusky Bay; between the cobbles
downtown, off 13th,
where aging softball players tee up,
rip golfballs off a corregated cat-walk, a warehouse,
watch them land on the roof of the Trailways
Bus Terminal. It speaks in every bottle, there

on the sidewalk; in Ralph,
the bartender's lisp, inside,
    "Crist, wat asshoes,"
as he speaks to the old-timer,
the one who once asked me
up to his room, told me I could try
on some of his new clothes.

persecution (the hundredth sheep)

I have heard their voices,
every one.

But You, who have been my Father,
my share,
shall ever be.

Outside these gates...

Accept this belled sheep,
    this dark kitchen dweller.

Second Coming

I catch Patrick, locked in, dimmed in amazement,
watching his mother and me, both tight as pistol shots
during a tense, second half replay.

His smile lets me know I'm too late and
I wonder, what intelligence has he gathered?
Siblings maybe, the face we share,
or what we were like, running through ancient streets.

And then leaving, I glimpsed Carly in the tub:
a three year old, singing a soft, almost mournful tune,
with suds, the top of a yellow plastic sugar bowl
on her head.

If they should die before we wake,
I wonder, what would be lost?

repentance

Slowly
incense rises,
an altarboy, hidden
in the ringing of his bells.

Your will is food
for a pool of hermits, locked,
lanced, in a graze of desert:
wild wheat, warm honey.

Hide and Seek (Ontario)

Holy One, You cannot hide.
I see You, imbedded, above western pines,
in the late morning, razor blue sky.

You laugh, sit
on punctual pines where snow gathers
graciously to the ground; on bushes, pounds of thick
sculpted hats, shifting shawls, the stinging beads
of white.

You lurk amid the red hair of the birch
(a pure mutiny!), in new water where, more than once,
I've addled in my canoe.

I could tell everyone,
but this cold trumpet, this bright note,
how can I play it
until You stop singing?

Our Father

Glory to the Father
Who guideth His children with a tender hand,
Who watches over the hay-bailers,
and to Whom the cricket sings.
He is like the stars and the broad rivers
that move beneath them.
He is like Paris or Rome.
He is like taxes.

He forgeth the metal in the fire,
the birds fly from His singing,
glows at the end of the day.

Who is there to visit Him?
Who to bring Him mirrors?

Hyperbole

Praise the Lord
Who loveth the fat man,
for he is jocund.
Who loveth the beetle and the amoeba
for they are universes
unto themselves.
Who maketh the round ball
and the skinny hole.

He is the milk and sap
of our dispositions, the red arm,
the other shoe. We walk
for hours behind Him,
losing our way,
losing our way.

Once

I, too, get to go through it.
Hallowed halls, like all those
before me: St. Peter,
Little Sister Amen, every duck,
ostrich.

Will there be paintings on the wall?
A "St. Francis slept here"?
I think they'll be an old couch or two,
Tommy Dorsey records.
The carpet won't be much,
but I'm going barefoot.

And the moment before!
My body serving its eviction notice,
the last absurd look at a dresser, wall;
the tears of a friend.

Versailles

Others
are kind enough to remind you.
They see you clearly,
the things you lack.
Their labored attention is a bellboy
carrying bags, an old hood, shiny,
its silver ornament.
They are instruments
of your youth.

Soon you will be able to walk barefoot
down the halls of Versailles.
If you are lucky,
they will throw you out.

Moon

Psalm #42

In the woods,
behind a dark tangle, the blackened arms of trees,
in the deer's rhythmic, bough-like chew,
its hooves, lies the cold
creak of the stream.

Moon overhead and
through the rakes of trees move
the parched, wasted corn stalks,
the snow clouds.

A colder wind calls through the wet,
slacking limbs.

My hands clam deep in the soil,
fingers pressed years beneath the earth.
My head hangs like a gourd.

In the red veins of the beets, Indian
arrowheads, winging
geese. And at night, in the stars,
the slow sway in the tall thicket, the blue
moon and first broad flakes.

Winter

The blue salt crunches on the platform
after a day of banging jaws:
the strap of a freight elevator,
of packing display signs into thin boxes,
fingerprints worn in the handling
of cold cardboard. Just the three of us
and aisles of pallets, neatly stacked
in the cavernous warehouse.

I watch cars underneath hunker down
in the bitter cold,
hear the slow, sure grind of
frozen rubber inching over treads of snow.
The cars seem to weigh each movement
—energy expended. Through
wisps of monoxide,
they speak grudgingly, and even then,
only when spoken to; the cold road, the nearby steel,
each bitter as breakdown.

Eels of snow rattle chain link fences,
burn our faces, exposed wrists.
Each of us, tramping on the platform,
huddling in his or her coat until, finally,
the rails ring: broken, cold,
as the lights in the dusk search them out:
spent variations under years of weight, speed;
and the snow, flurrying before that train,
with its welcome, if artificial, heat.

Christmas Night Cab Stand
(Ft. Collins, Co.)

Jupiter, in the early evening
shines like Bethlehem
over the crescent;
pale blue, the moon's northeastern side.

Earlier,
the mist in front of the foothills,
the foothills themselves,
both, colored slate as the last light
worked its way down through the clouds, the peaks.

Scraggy cottonwoods, distant,
could have been palms.
And the condos, nearer,
seemed to rise up out of soft brown earth.

Another Christmas, and what is born here
has made the sky its own, given
words to every tree.

Marian Sector

Wet boots, a slightly packed snow field,
trees glazed, under a grey sky.
Streaks, finger-painted clouds, ground
to woodchuck ground.
Flakes begin to fall,
thick now, as a Rambler over deep
snow.
The young trees are bare, sticks,
or your life,
who they are.
You touch them, with sweaty hands,
having taken off your layered mitts:
the deerskin, the wool.
The bark is rough, slick,
seems to cut at your fingers.

You pass.

*

In the morning, when the sun
has taken its fill from tall crystal,
flowers, from gutters,
and rises, half drunk, like a cowboy
in the Hand which holds it,

and you find yourself alone, again,
at breakfast, face deep in pollen,
drowning; alive as the
white sword is drawn from its pink sheath:
your heart.

She is there, with you,
looking out past the curtains
to the stars and the roundness of the sea.

*

To possess nothing,
all of it.

This is your end.
To feel yourself rise in conversation,
ignore it,
go on talking.
          To become so small
          that there is finally room
          for you
          on the sidewalk.

*

See your hands; they
are not
yours.
Move then, in silence,
hidden among the towers,
the loud talkers, along the shoreline—
frisbees, sun bathers.
What is yours, no one
else wants. What is yours,
is yours
alone.

*

The leaves fall.
They must.

So, how often, our own faces
are downcast, having howled
as we do, like beasts
in a reddening void,
having received instead,
winter fields, the breath of horses.

*

I saw an old woman today
downtown, and though I'm sure no one else
noticed, there was, I am positive,
a small flame which flickered
on the top of her head.

She was pushing a cart of groceries.
As I came closer to her car, bent on inspecting,
she handed me a sack of potatoes.

Before she drove away, she smiled,
and, insisted, pressing
two warn quarters
against my palm.

*

The plain wooden statue, and on the way up
to Communion, on the left cheek,
I saw a tear glistening.

She is a door
that signals procession,
the kind you feel, sometimes, mornings,
stopping your bicycle in a
graveyard, each person, one day,
rising, walking eastward
through cold grass,
dissipating mist.

You will be among them.

*

Beaded tears
on grotto floors.
We recite them, drone, as if at a funeral,
count our sins, the days we left
on the road to Sodom,
the days of wheat and barley,
of fast talking, back slapping.

They are our cry, they are
her answer.
We do not know what is to come;
we know, what is here.

OUT OF AFRICA

Walking back, college guys, decibels
rising with the adolescent competition.
And later, college girls across the street, giggling,
singing a few lines, belching, about beer.

I want to push them all out, away.
I want to hold the dark ruby of being alone,
move in it, in the dim fins of light
on the night wall, feel its water.
I want to bear its red tone
until morning.

So I walk, a country road, two miles
out of town, surrounded by pale stalks,
the occasional patch of snow, to a place,
a hike from any house, under
stars. I sit
down on that unlined road, look up
from where my home is, until a chill
begins to wrap my legs.

Room

In my bed at night,
unable to sleep,
with a train outside
rumbling past,
shaking the frame of this rented house,
        and I'm a child again,
        knowing I only have so many
        of these breaths to my name,
        so many heartbeats.

I wasn't afraid,
only struck by the oddness of it,
a body which, like a name,
never seemed to catch it.

"Train," I say,
and go to sleep.

Joseph in the Dungeon

He must have learned the most
in the hours when he could not pray,
sitting there, waiting for
nothing to happen, with the
knowledge that his plans
were only that, and
that the water dripping
was the measure of his life
being taken.

He must have been awed
at the absolute conciseness
of the spider: wrapping, weaving.
Maybe orange light, high above,
moved reddening, on clear days,
up the wall. He must have learned
to sit for hours until, at last,
he learned how much a hireling was worth,
how much, his royal blood.

Gethsemani

Damp wind, the innocent
movement of grubs at the roots of trees.

The moon, a moth
caught fluttering in wet branches:
       white wings, slowing.

Then the angel, gathering
the pieces of Jesus, large hand caressing His head,
the rumpled folds of hair
to his chest, blood on the snow white gown.
       The slow, unearthly movement
       of giant wings.

He cried out, for the ones to follow:
       ...in a haze He saw
bodies, twistings in a thin
dark oil. Voices, the sucking
of flesh away from flesh, the relapse.
       Waves of voices, in time:
Abraham's lament, Napoleon
cursing in the snow, the rumble of horses.
A cut-off arm in high weeds, box lunch
of Kentucky Fried, the spiked sound
of the Avon lady, her heels up the walk...

Litany

Mother of Sorrow,
Mother of stars and night fires, arroyos,
tossed tequila bottles,
the dead drunk.
Mother of the streets, of the violent,
weekend golfers, cut off,
and a windshield smashed with bare fists;
the knife, the absurdity, the day in court.
Mother of amphetamines, the aging
speed freak, who looks to kick
around an oval track in a beat up
stock car. Mother of the subways,
the swaying lost.
Mother of day laborers, children,
early mornings, in the fields.
Mother of Guatemala,
of empty Ohio River steel towns
where no more black soot seeps
into the cracks of the houses.
Mother of Cleveland, of every neon bar,
honky tonk. Mother of Hank Williams,
late night pick-ups that end in
anguish or bruises.
Mother of every redneck,
alone and crossed at closing,
every liberal who circles a silo
in protest, crying out
to be loved.

"Christ Bearing the Cross"
by El Greco

The honey-red hue of the picture,
along with the eyes (left one, wetter),
suggest the greater temptation:
the prospect of creation, evidence of God's love,
breaking apart.

There is no logic here. Only
loss. That face, bruised, is calm.
The calm. The red in the cloak, the sky
is also blood, suggested.
The body that was of earth, the earth
changed.

    Bright red berries
    in the fall. How here, in western Ohio,
    the whole sodden scene becomes
    tinted. A tree brimming, and yet,
    bare. Red leaves among the fallen brown,
    yellow. Grey sky, trees, the whole
    terrible fecundity,
    as if the earth were too loaded, too late.

His neck is thick, masculine.
His shoulders, too broad, long muscle somehow
speaking an unhurried pace.
The hands, in contrast, are delicate. The left one,
down the cross He not so much bears
as becomes, toward the bottom of the painting.
Only the smallest finger, almost an afterthought,
crooked, notes Hell's harrowing.

Fixed, submissive. He wears an angular halo.
A geometry of wood, and the clouds
opening above the cross' raised arm, which might,
from this frontal view (the long beam, across His back,
hidden), easily, wittily, be the top,
instead, of a
smaller cross.

Pastoral

The morning rain that washes clean the leaves,
washes the tongue. Old words, stories,
gone in green and light
through the white edges of
grey clouds, light which shines
on beads of rain, waxed leaves.

Walking barefoot, wet sand.
Unconsciously, I grab an overhanging branch,
am showered, and, on the sidestep,
soaked. Long green spears of grass angle
under pantleg, against my bone-white ankle.

*

The brook I had expected in not here;
neither did I walk to arrive.
In anger, surging, the white river
stretches its harness.
Its bestial back, brown, convex, at mid-river,
its flanks muscling against the splayed green,
along overnanging banks carries
the stone I toss. It splashes ten feet down river.

*

44

The volleyball net is something to hold on to,
encased in tires and cement.
The keg is tapped; there are summer cherries,
all the latest cheeses,
lawn chairs and grass thick enough
to spread your toes in.

After a game, over beers, I talk with
Rita about Quaker Services, with
Bill and Nancy about hiking the divide;
Vicki, Robin, and Lester. We talk Bar Mitzvahs,
Presbyterian Confirmations, rites of passage.
Our "Yeas" and "Nays," birds, twittering
in season, or columbines which cup in the pre-dawn,
laid bare by an afternoon sun.

                    *

The smell of rain is an auger.
A few drops and soon the street is flooded
clean. From the porch hammock
I hear the crack and recrack of thunder, children
squealing under lightning and the pavement, alive
and crowded with hail.

Spray and leaves soon win the porch.
Inside, new to gardening, I look out back,
see the tropical leaves, my huge zucchinis trampled,
wonder if they will survive.
A week later, with new leaves, I see they have.

*

THE MONKS OF MOUNT TABOR
AND THE
Ukraniec family invite you to
celebrate with them the
Ordination

of Br. Michael (Nickolas)

TO THE PRIESTHOOD OF CHRIST BY THE
GRACE OF THE HOLY SPIRIT AND AT THE
HANDS OF BISHOP INNOCENT LOTOCKY OF
THE EPARCHY OF CHICAGO...

HOLY YEAR PILGRIMMAGE AND
picnic immediately following
Ordination

*

What picnic with friends and relations,
blankets spread out by the duck pond,
could coax the echo of the "yea" that rings through
high firs?

When you, Father, look down over that
redwood porch railing,
down through the valley some night,
say a prayer for us,
that our mouths might be dark as the sky
and our words seldom as stars.

Mulberry Leaves

Late summer flaps in clouds
over the green little town,
its shiny cars, its mannequin dreams,
has taken the children,
left them, in tall grass on the hill,
where the stars will all fall like mulberry leaves
and the moon bob on the spine of the sea.

Poem begun while
listening to Beethoven's EROICA

Red rectangles, an aurora
across the night sky.

A mouse, its tracks;
great, high limbs creaking,
the wind shaking loose packed snow:
heavy white birds and wisps, a
layer of powder, dissolving
into night.

There are lights on up into the mountains
and everywhere, against the stations
of cathedral steeps, hearths and loved ones.
The crackle of brandy, the piling of
seasons.

*

The snow falls and falls, for days.
You wake to a cold stove,
ash under the handled plates.

You split kindling,
warm yourself on the small cot,
lean back against the curve of log, the
chinking. A votive candle flickers on the wall
below an icon.

49

And at the window, from across the snow,
stands of grass, no loved one.
Only the days, the walks. . .

Inside, a kerosene lamp,
a book and the knowledge that
this, too, as you sit, is passing.

*

A shifting of air currents along the tree line,
a few rocks, slide and
the steady, healing sound of water.

Lower, boys light matches
beneath the tall arms of trees.
In town, a horsedrawn wagon rumbles over
cobblestones in front of lit shopwindows,
open late, for the season.

Winter clouds, pale, diaphonous,
overhead.

*

Red rectangles again, in front of the
trunks of trees, above the icy edges,
the movement in the dark stream.

Static in the cold night air, a march:
thousands of miniature soldiers on the dimly
lit snow. Night, in the rocks, in
a long-dead mammalian species which
forages, eons ago, along these waters.

In a lone house, ten miles away, someone,
each night, all night,
leaves the lights on.

*

Here, in a starry field, are horses.
A half drunk soldier embraces four of them over
a barbed-wire fence. He is talking
to God. And then the silence,
the horses.

*

Most of us are called
to wait—

Angels over moonlit snow
like large moths or very old
children. They sport in pure idleness;
two grave diggers, with shovels
over their shoulders, trudge, knee-deep,
share the laughter, the shine
in a cold, silver flask.

*

51

Onto uplifted palms
the snow falls. Though we know the way
to the onion-topped chapel in the woods,
the path takes us away from artificial light,
darkens. We listen for
other voices.

The main house waits with a feast
that will last all night.
Some people I don't know will play
foreign instruments and friends will talk
for hours, in the wild flickering
of candlelight.

*

Let the planets revolve, the One I love
idles, earphones on, across the room.

*

These nights I spend
collecting stars from the river,
walking to an early sun, low, over the snow,
I don't know what they mean.
I don't know whom I help.

Music moves in heavy boot,
in tides, cold organs: northern seas,
and on them, flakes falling.

Two eggs jiggle, ogle from the stove.

So let me walk then, like the skid row
husker of brown bags, looking out
from a bed of shredded pallets,
his nearly toothless smile,
wide as rabbit tracks.

So let me walk, red rectangles
on the back shoulder of my coat.

So let me walk.

Downtown Steubenville
"The end of everything
is the love of Jesus crucified."
Charles de Foucauld

In a basin of rust-colored leaves,
a valley of old stoves;
in shells of cut brick, houses,
brushed in black leaf: broken window eye;
down patched alleys, thin as a way home,
where a young black boy flips
a garbage bag, engages
in tentative rat sport.

10 am:
a man seated on cement steps,
head in his hands, rises,
walks to the heel of the building
and rejects; the smell of wine
drifts down the asphalt.

2 am:
cabstand, a man leans, urinates,
closer to the street than to the alley.
Down in front of the Imperial Hotel,
a woman shouts, struggles to get free.
Her man stands full stature in front of her and soon
they are, again, in each other's arms.

Linda (the last to know)

1)
In the twilight
your dimming green rooms
wait: old lamps, one wall covered
in antique photos, frames.
Muted lights
slide across the wall.
I wait;
the quiet night
sleeves.

2)
Clear-Eyed Bell,
your ringing escapes
you. Soaked in wine, on your couch,
stomach, glasses slightly askew,
mouth, working,
bent by the cushion,
your shoe dangles
off an elevated foot
as, carefully,
you sub-divide.

for Paige

This woman I like,
she drives a red car with headlights
that flip up.
The seats, too, are red
and black, and the dash,
all lights and graphs.
She puts in a casette of Indian chants,
sings alone. She is a lawyer.
I try to keep all this away from me,
remain myself. She talks sweat-lodges,
Indian healing, about how she had to sit outside
because it was her time of the month.
She talks about her sacred pipe,
the one she found waiting for her
in Phoenix.

This is music.

*

I surprised her, walked over Sunday night.
She took me out back, showed me
the circle of stones in the grass
behind the garage. She instructed me,
and we smoked the pipe,
touching it to earth after pointing it,
four directions.

Before I left, I held her.
Through the robe, her welcome thatch,
the responsibility of pleasing.

*

The day after the anger,
leaving her at the restaurant,
as I waited for my boss to come outside,
I saw a sick bird quake on his driveway;
before that, walking to work,
someone had left a dishevelled doll, standing, muddy,
in her front yard.

The bird blinked, the insides
of its eyes were white and stood out
against its dark feathers.
The doll had mud in its hair,
all over its legs, and the next day,
was face down in the mud.

I called you at work, left a message,
never heard.
We are poor healers, you and I.
When called on most to listen, we hear
the least.
Hear me now.
I want to see you.

After FRAGMENTS OF MY LIFE
(by Catherine Doherty)

What Russian Valentino was this?
Necklace in his almost smooth hands, announcing,
"We are ruined."

What stock, anointing his naked wife
with Gethsemani's oil
before the children, all night begging, "Lord,
save my wife"?

I think of how little I've valued women,
women who either high-heeled into a monastery
printing room, or who came more quietly,
a hand on my shoulder, from behind,
while I was seated in church;
women who were potters,
or makers of teeth, whose souls were so deep,
that when I prayed with them,
I felt like a bird flying above an abyss,
or whose spirits were so ascetic
that I became nauseated at the hint of locust,
desert air; or this woman, whose laughter is a thin glass
for her pain. She sits at the piano
and belts out hymn after hymn. A true Methodist,
she sings loud and on key; then she
tokes and calls Jesus
by his Indian name.

                    Each
from God's hand, each worthy
of being seen for what she is:
a glimpse of eternity. Worth a necklace
or any other material thing.

A sick man's hands
(after C. K. Williams)

I only began to really notice her the second time I saw
her crying on her front steps next door as, again,
I walked past. I wondered why she chose to
so obviously, publicly, show her pain to me.

When she first introduced herself a week before,
I shook her hand, noticed the waver in her smile.
The tenuousness of it frightened me. I felt that if I
squeezed harder, her hollow hand, her whole hollow body
would shatter right there, and I'd be left
with pieces of plastic. In my hands. On her doorstep.

It's so typical of God.
You're lost, angry at the whole gender,
and what does He do? Drops a wounded woman in front of
    you.

When she asked me to move some concrete,
I walked through a spare living room. Two thinning green
50s cardboard chairs huddled in a corner.
A rail thin lamp. Past a slight, holly-farm kitchen,
a Bible, opened on the table, into her backyard.

It was another world. Bright green. Exterior.
With carpet grass, decorative rock.
I'd seen her there often, watched her shear the leaves
off hedges, heard her hands in the spaces
between yard and walk.

After I finished, we sat and talked for a long time
in her living room. I watched as her lower lids
slowly filled with water. The tics in her smile.
She pointed to her husband's picture. Dead at 32.
Cancer. She said when she first saw me on the street,
she thought he'd come back to life.

I stayed away, against my back ribs, talked
about Jesus, about how He works in the natural.
Gave her numbers of support groups, told her
about a church in town where you could feel the Spirit
from the sidewalk.

In the months that followed, she would invite me over.
We'd watch TV, play Scrabble. I learned
about her history of depression, electroshock treatments,
the dead child, all of the living ones
on the Western slope with her first husband.

From a measured distance,
I saw her slowly, with gathering strength, rise,
start a daycare center. A baby
on each hip, singing in the front yard.

I moved about three weeks ago at
four in the morning. Believe still, that somehow, God
used me. And last Thursday, on the Cathedral steps
downtown, I saw an old lady sitting, massaging her red,
elephantine, rashed leg. Slowly,
slowly, with vasoline.

Nursing Home, 3rd Shift
(after C. K. Williams)

This one guy who had recently been brought in,
having had his first heart attack. Feisty. He'd
slug you when you tried to change his diaper, ("Depends"
they called them), as you tried to remove the mound
of shit, the smear, wipe his ass, the back of his
balls.
      And Horace. Stately, small,
a former factory worker. He'd cry out "Pee-pee, pee-pee"
whenever you passed him, making rounds. How
when you took him to the bathroom, you'd have
to shuffle along side of him, your hands under his elbows
(I'd sometimes make noises like a train).
Mornings he dressed easy, but you wondered if he'd just
be sitting on that couch all day, waiting for meals,
movement.
      Charlie was ambulatory, loved
the Tigers, his old Japanese transistor radio
pressed to his ear, in front of the TV,
catching the late game from the coast.
He could only mumble, but was happy.
That year they won the pennant.
      There was an old lady
who used to talk non-stop whenever you potted her.
She talked about the town's long gone Heinz plant,
about her family's history. All in one long,
continuous monologue. The other two women:

                                                    Joanie,
too old to talk, with a little girl's smile.
She had been a teacher, liked her sock doll
with her when, in the mornings, I'd strap
her into her all-day chair. The straps were soft, padded,
and the early morning, women workers, cheerful.
            The other one, Mary,
was the owner's mother, and loved it when I, a man, dressed
            her.

I quit though. Work hours cut in half
without notice, tired of going home, smelling
of urine. It struck me, how much
they were like most people, living because,
ultimately, they liked it. Maybe they
were an unusual bunch. But it seemed good for
them. Babies again, in diapers.
Getting changed and touched a lot. People digging them,
not because of what they brought to a conversation,
but because they were alive.

            And for me,
no matter what I'm doing now, it always seems the same:
trying to learn to do the little thing well,
trying to, as the Moslems say, remember;
to learn how to be there, serve, each time, maybe,
getting a little closer to where
I want to be.

**for McVey, in the wake
of her murdered lover** (after C. K. Williams)

Linda,
yesterday I took the Shaker Rapid after a day of painting.
Speckles in my hair. When this beautiful woman,
some stops later got on I felt, as I often do, wounded
in spirit. Wondered why that was.

And then today I began thinking
about my ex-fiancee, Liza, and was filled with
sorrow, remorse. Wondered who was the crueler.
Searching for some consolation, some word,
I picked up a Billy Graham thought-for-a-day book.
Finding nothing there I started, arbitrarily, to read the
Bible. Samuel. I was struck by David's gentleness.
His heart. How openhanded he was. Weeping for his
defeated dead son, Absolom, and then, curbing that for
the sake of his victorious troops.

I became aware of my own heart. How it
often is like that. Full of the gentleness
that comes only from God. I saw that it was like
David's, because, and to the extent that,
it was broken. It also became clear why it must,
on some level, remain that way.

I hope that some of this is helpful to you
in your grief. I hope that you turn to God who will
be your refuge, who calls and turns
even the blackest sorrow
into joy.

Photograph

Sometimes when I see my face in the mirror,
I see my father's
in an iron lung.

He looks right at the camera,
says, "This is what it is:
life, something that directs YOU,
out of your hands.
Just when you think
you can skate, pockets out and empty
down easy street,
God opens your eyes, lets you see that
you're only carrying your body,
lets you see
it bleed.
Look at me."

A few of his teeth missing, and I know,
in the mirror,
that I'm not young anymore, hope
that when it's all done, put away,
someone still living, can look at me
and say, simply, "Yes."

the dance (for Maurice)

Yesterday, in the library,
I sat listening to Vivaldi, earphones on,
while in the corner of the large room,
on TV, they began to roll the tape
back and forth. The shuttle's
final minute. The glow
between it and the fuel tank:
the whitening, dimming, whitening.
With a priest's joy
in my ears I watched a day-old
interview. A woman crew member,
and like so many times this year,
I felt it: the time alotted, to
people, to the buildings on Main Street
outside the window.
I thought of our conversation.
Your impression of having your heart stop,
as, fully conscious, you lay there on the couch,
agitation increasing with the minutes as
you waited for it to start beating again.
Lately it's all been so clear for me.
How one day I'll be like the woman
being interviewed, full of pride and
expectation, and then, somewhere else.
The whole world, too, could end
as you lean over your dirty stove,
fry a hamburger.

St. Francis called her Sister Death.
Lorca, something else. And it's true.
She's the one you dance with,
the one who leans on your shoulder
as you write. And though I see the
fear she inspires on freshmen faces,
I welcome her. When my time comes,
I want to meet her in these old clothes,
on this street. I will be
standing there, and my body will
leave me. I will dance my quiet dance,
wait for someone to come.

the Apprentice

Becoming Apprentice

Like hawks, outside of time,
perched on the limbs of the seasons,
I walk past these big old houses, their lights.
They settle in, under snow, trees.

A little boy shovels with his dad.
He can't lift what he has gathered,
falls to his knees.
His father is silent. Perhaps he, too,
hears it: the night.
The sprigs, feathers, sprouting
neatly up his back.

He'll want to move away
from the warmth,
become apprentice to the cold,
creaking wheels of the planets,
the iced necks of stars.

Inviting Winter

Come, winter,
with your cheeks your
furtive gusts;
slow to writing
in the trees,
the almost-stilled lake.
Beneath old ones, tributaries
of bark, I leap,
bound from the rocks.
I find a river,
heave a stone,
listen for the great dunking,
walk home.

Come, lordly times, times
of purest grotesquery:
two boot dances
in the high snow,
an existential bellow
over a field.

The clouds answer
as they always do.
The earth turns,
and, because I am lucky,
I will return
until I am gone.

Christmas with Ed* and the Remote Control

I hear a clicking,
a small sound like wind
from the radiator,
from outside.

It's dark now,
and the apartments below mine, empty.
The TV—with every local high school choir,
a nice production of "A Child's Christmas in Wales,"
parts of three Scrooge and Marley's, a flock of
*It's a Wonderful Life*s and *Miracles on 34th Street*,
both in faded color and black and white,
Pavoratti, in costume, and then, on another channel,
in tux, Loretta Swit in Germany,
3 French hens and Flordia versus UCLA—
off.

I am alone
with what is left of Christmas—
a solitude to match the season   outside,
a sharp bark in the white distance,
the slapping together of cold deerskin mitts,
my breath climbing and nothing
but cold, pilgrim stars
to steer the weather by.
*the dog

73

The Apprentice is Amazed

Oh, for the holiness which is a needle
and all the space it leaves in a wine glass;
Glass! Clear and fragile as cement mixers
——a topic for discussions!
Everything transient, like Reeboks,
the holes in your jeans.

Everywhere in my life, people are leaving.
Except in the crowded department stores,
chandeliers glistening near the ceiling.
This is what there is!
Salami, a cold orange with its incredible juices.
Who would have thought life
was going to contain that!

The Apprentice Rejoices

Verily, spring hath come,
and there is goodness in the land.
Everywhere, the snows recede,
everywhere, the sound of running water.

Our little sisters, the plants,
bustle over unmade beds, morning.
Mice stretch in the fields.
(Their little couches are dusty
from the long winter.)
People start going to church.

And the frosted blade who started all this—
he's joyful, forgotten.

The Apprentice Wavers

What about the green stems
that hide inside the earth?
What about THEM?
Do you think they go on eating
as if nothing has happened?!
Some kind of cow in the brown earth!
Look. They are as abuzz as the cold water
dripping from the roof, as an
algebra book on the road.

Every earthly thing shared your joy
when you got new tires on your car.
And why not?
The planet is more than dirt.
It's true. Everything has already happened!
All you have to do is be still.
Put some clothes on,
wait to fill them.

Get me a beer.
We will flap in the breeze.

Apprentice as Columbo

These yellow roses
which trundle next to the house
are wearing overcoats!
They look like Columbo,
musing, waving their arms.

I stand in front of them,
do the same.
But it's no use.
It would never work out.

Down the street a squirrel
rips up someone's clean sod,
finding winter nuts.
I'm grateful for the chaos.
It restoreth my soul,
leads me to still water.

Nothing is as it seems!
The lawn's ways are not the squirrel's.
And the whole damn thing
rides on the night.

the Apprentice Eats Glass

Your friend, the end, comes every day:
doorbells and flowers.
He eats your grass, spackles your chimney.
Let him. He is your guest.

Invite him to sit on the porch
to share your melon, spit the seeds.
Barefoot, the two of you can collect
the dirt from between your toes,
use it against yourselves,
become halls of angry voices.

Tell him the red razor
scratches you where you itch.

He'll get serious for a moment,
tell you the radical laws of departure
are everywhere in evidence, everywhere
a bus stops on the corner of Hollywood and time.
Join in the fun.
Tell him that half the passengers there
are dead, but to ignore them,
there is little they can say.

the Apprentice Sees Himself in the Sunset

The lepers grew excited
beneath my window this morning,
danced like Carmen Miranda,
or a band at the Holiday Inn.

Almost immediately,
I had a vision on Third Street, a pietá:
Mother Teresa held Jimmy Swaggert.
Some kids, off to the side, were laughing,
and I heard the sound of a basketball settling,
for a second, in the chain net while the sky
seemed like some fragile instrument
made entirely of glass.

Break it
whenever you can. The slivers
stuck in your throat
might save you from speaking.

Graceful Exit

The rat-tailed lobsters
who sit in high chairs,
in bibs, eat crayfish
in the clack clacking of their jaws,
juices dribbling down scaley chins.

It IS probably enough to say one's sorry,
to regret our claws,
hold them, in shame, behind our backs;
to feel, as the front of our chair is removed,
the depths of our plated natures;
to feel the grace,
the mud we flop in;
to warm to garbage.
It's enough to feel the cold blood pulse
at our throats, to crawl
self-consciously across the floor
with that slight side-to-side motion,
the one that makes us feel,
if only for a moment,
like seals.
It's good to listen closely to the tac-tac sounds
our claws make on the tiles,
as people move chairs to make way;
to see an antenna occasionally
bob before us
as we try to hold up a good front,

march boldly through
our secretions
toward the door.

the Apprentice Considers Fleas

The flea on your bed at night
has such tiny feet! He treks in moonlight
across white dunes.
The buzz of his feelers occupies
all of his attention.
He seldom gives a thought
for his brother who is in Timbuktu
or for the rice on the kitchen floor.
And the moon! It is there
and bathes him in such light!
He could almost stop,
grab a cigaret.
But does he? No I tell you.
He marches on, down a ravine,
across a leg.

Stop the murder.
Stop it.

New Age

Under early streetlight
frozen leaves are stacked
like corpses
or Russian cordwood,
the Ayatollah's honeymoon.
They weave their frosted spell
in Central America,
in the continual hum of "the starry dynamo,"
in garden tillers, kneading soil,
limbs. Death gurgles in the mold.
Earth people! Every step toward the soil!

I met a new hippy downtown the other day,
sure of his gentle nature,
proclaiming consciousness, a new order.
One man in a wilderness.
It had better watch out.

A Capella

If you want the truth,
you must look for it.
It's that simple.
If it's there, it will stick a foot out
as you pass; he will hold his side laughing
as you fall. Like an insurance salesman
from Nebraska.

It will be more than you expected.

But then, of course, you must decide
what you're going to do with him.
He might follow you into the Deli,
maybe say something about the Jews.
You can just picture him
down on the corner with the boys,
trying to fit in, over the fire
in the evenings,
with his wide-open polyester suit,
his white belt (your friends will hate him
but won't be able to ask him to leave
because of his size). He'll try to sing
the bass part, completely destroy the harmony.

No sir,
you won't be able to take him anywhere.

the Apprentice in his Groove

The best days
aren't worth counting.
They go by without notice
or event, an easy shuffle between brain songs
and ladder marks on the sides of houses.
I am content with a well drawn ceiling line,
getting the right amount of paint on mullions, windows.
And, in the heat, lunch:
a Big Mac and a coke,
cold as the shower waiting
at home.

In the evening, take in a ballgame,
sit in the sparsely crowded
upper reserves.
Pick a seat where you can put your feet up,
marvel at how white the bases are
as your cousin talks about Kant.

A breeze will come in off the lake,
dry your hair,
and you'll be glad you're in Cleveland.

an Apprentice goes to a Prayer Meeting

May birds fly from my mouth
if I speak with another tongue.
Let this stew kettle, fire,
these truck tracks, mud ruts and
standing water speak for us.
What we need are better hammers,
more nails.
Then if our crops fail,
it will be on our heads.

Do what you're going to,
wait around for the day that will come,
but don't hand me a stone,
call it a fish.

I'll pick grass for my teeth
every time. I'll walk the road in wet boots,
be thankful for the rain.

the Apprentice Prophecies

It's the wreath you don't come upon
in a snowy field some grey morning,
the few remaining strands
of tinsil, moving in the cold.
And days later, the cabin nearer
the horizon, light through the shades,
a chilly sky before dawn.

It's your steel porch rail in sunlight
beneath the mailboxes: bright, flat black,
the brick behind. You'll be struck dumb
by the ordinary, and everything
will start to matter:
what shirt you put on,
how to pronounce your name.

You'll start helping dogs across the street,
be careful not to cycle over worms
after rain. You and the whole neighborhood,
everyone with quick, uncertain wheels.
Hand brakes and balance. You'll come home hours later,
muddy, but happy.

You'll keep waiting for it to end.

the Apprentice Considers his Addiction

I'm slick as Vermont maple.
After a shower I grease my wet hair back,
check my aquiline nose.

I make cameo appearances
at 7-11s,
eat little powdered donuts
in the back of the store,
get the white stuff of wisdom
on my beard.

I am your brother, mother;
I am the socks in your drawer:
a sprawl of ganglia, nerve-endings,
and I WILL go out with your daughter.

So, if on the street, I offer you
one of my marshmellows,
eat quickly through the pale skin,
catch the gooey center where the mercury is pure.
There you'll find all the cars,
all the traffic in the world.

Give me your granules, not your love.
A pound of confectioners.
We can go out into the desert.
Bounce among the ruins.

the Apprentice Muses Matrimonial

I wanna meet me
some nice Franciscan woman—
long-suffering, patient,
the kind who don't like money.

I can put my feet up on some old
dusty ottoman, in a house without rugs.
We would do our little jobs:
she hers, me mine.
Maybe raise up some kids,
runny noses, second hand clothes.

The whole family
could crawl in the window of my car
(the doors being permanently stuck).
We'd bundle in the winter,
put up a flap for the rain.

We'd make a scene just
walking through the supermarkets,
the plastic tips of shoelaces
making their little sounds on the tiles,
ten ruddy faces;
maybe we'd eat oranges right there
off the shelves.

the Fire on the Mountain

I collect gaskets—
all sizes, shapes. Hang them throughout
my apartment. They make lovely conversation pieces.
Make me feel so
—manual.

Everybody collects something.
I knew this one guy who collected snap cap
plastic bottles. Said they made him feel safe. He died,
looking over his left shoulder.

It's always like that.
One person or another dying,
someone's kid raiding your fridge or
sticking to your carpet.

None of it works.
You still have to go back:
bowling on Tuesdays, March winds,
the fire on the mountain.

the Apprentice Counsels a not-so-young Rilke

Li Po was every bit as foolish
as you. Basho, too,
could have been Curly,
nyuk, nyuking his way into the heart
of cold water.

So you have to walk the unpaved road
with your carpet bag,
the noises within.
Someone will pick you up.
You'll find work in Hattiesburg;
the grim reaper will deliver your mail.
Accept it all with some grace. Loosen
your shoe strings. Buy an old black and white.

The petals will float down the streams
in your living room.
You can watch all the ministers on TV,
open your windows as wide as you like.

the Apprentice Speaks of Retirement

Flee from the world.
Hide in its crevices,
in your baking cookies.

A friend will appear
off a Greyhound bus;
you'll have a few in an old bar
across the street.
You'll drive your rusted Toyota
home, where you'll swap stories, poems.
He'll fill you in on his divorce,
sleep on your floor.
In the morning
you'll drive him the last hundred miles.

No one will be the wiser.
You can walk the streets the next day,
buy a paper, some coffee.

About the Author

David Craig was born in Berea, Ohio in 1951. He is the author of three books of poetry: THE SANDALED FOOT (The Cleveland State University Poetry Center, 1980), PSALMS (Me First Press, 1982), and PETER MAURIN AND OTHER POEMS (The Cleveland State University Poetry Center, 1985). In addition, his poems have appeared in numerous periodicals as well as in the anthologies, THE WIDENING LIGHT (Harold Shaw Publishers, 1984) and in WRESTLING WITH THE ANGEL (Baker, Gwynn, eds.). He holds a BA from Cleveland State, an MA from Colorado State, an MFA from Bowling Green State, and currently teaches at the Franciscan University of Steubenville.

Howard McCord on LIKE TAXES

"LIKE TAXES, by David Craig, is an impressive book. In an age dominated by the secular and characterized by the pretentious and trivial, we are fortunate to have a book so rooted in authentic experience, and serious concern. Craig is eager for the fullness of the religious experience, but he does not let himself be deceived by the superficially religious. He is a subtle enought theologian to know that God hides in strange places, and reveals Himself as He wills, not as mortals might imagine. The best way to encounter Him is to get on with your life—driving cab, talking with friends, eating supper—and staying as alert as the hunter is for the deer. These are the hunter's poems."

Mary Crow on PETER MAURIN AND OTHER POEMS (CSU Poetry Center, '85):

"David Craig is an unusual poet—first because he writes religious poetry in our secular age and second, and more importantly, because the poetry he writes does not try to convert or shame. But while this poetry belongs to the tradition of celebratory and mystical religious poetry, it does not shun ordinary life or language and it does not avoid contact with sinners or the antipoetic. Nor does it make faith easy. It simply tries to say: Faith, yes, reality, yes, and hope, somehow."

Murray Bodo, O.F.M., on THE SANDALED FOOT (CSU Poetry Center, '80):

"...These poems are the story of that profound reconciliation which enables Francis and those sparrows who followed after to lie down with the lion and the snake and expose their feet to everything that is. Like Francis these poems are disarmingly simply and unassuming, but you may have to remove your shoes, and more, to read them."

Scripta Humanistica

Directed by
BRUNO M. DAMIANI
The Catholic University of America
COMPREHENSIVE LIST OF PUBLICATIONS *

1. Everett W. Hesse, *The "Comedia" and Points of View.* $24.50
2. Marta Ana Diz, *Patronio y Lucanor: la lectura inteligente "en el tiempo que es turbio."* Prólogo de John Esten Keller. $26.00
3. James F. Jones, Jr., *The Story of a Fair Greek of Yesteryear.* A Translation from the French of Antoine-François Prévost's *L'Histoire d'une Grecque moderne.* With Introduction and Selected Bibliography. $30.00
4. Colette H. Winn, *Jean de Sponde: Les sonnets de la mort ou La Poétique de l'accoutumance.* Préface par Frédéric Deloffre.   out of print
5. Jack Weiner, *"En busca de la justicia social: estudio sobre el teatro español del Siglo de Oro."* $24.50
6. Paul A. Gaeng, *Collapse and Reorganization of the Latin Nominal Flection as Reflected in Epigraphic Sources.* Written with the assistance of Jeffrey T. Chamberlin. $24.00
7. Edna Aizenberg, *The Aleph Weaver: Biblical, Kabbalistic, and Judaic Elements in Borges.* $25.00
8. Michael G. Paulson and Tamara Alvarez-Detrell, *Cervantes, Hardy, and "La fuerza de la sangre."* $25.50
9. Rouben Charles Cholakian, *Deflection/Reflection in the Lyric Poetry of Charles d'Orléans: A Psychosemiotic Reading.* $25.00
10. Kent P. Ljungquist, *The Grand and the Fair: Poe's Landscape Aesthetics and Pictorial Techniques.*   out of print
11. D.W. McPheeters, *Estudios humanísticos sobre la "Celestina."* $20.00
12. Vittorio Felaco, *The Poetry and Selected Prose of Camillo Sbarbaro.* Edited and Translated by Vittorio Felaco. With a Preface by Franco Fido. $25.00
13. María del C. Candau de Cevallos, *Historia de la lengua española.* $33.00
14. *Renaissance and Golden Age Studies in Honor of D.W. McPheeters.* Ed. Bruno M. Damiani.   out of print
15. Bernardo Antonio González, *Parábolas de identidad: Realidad interior y estrategia narrativa en tres novelistas de postguerra.* $28.00

44. *Feminine Concerns in Contemporary Spanish Fiction by Women*. Edited by Roberto C. Manteiga, Carolyn Galerstein and Kathleen McNerney. $35.00
45. Pierre L. Ullman, *A Contrapuntal Method For Analyzing Spanish Literature*. $41.50
46. Richard D. Woods, *Spanish Grammar and Culture Through Proverbs*. $35.00
47. David G. Burton, *The Legend of Bernardo del Carpio. From Chronicle to Drama*. Preface by John Lihani. $30.00
48. Godwin Okebaram Uwah, *Pirandellism and Samuel Beckett's Plays*. $28.00
49. *Italo-Hispanic Literary Relations*, ed. J. Helí Hernández. $33.00
50. *Studies in Honor of Elias Rivers*, eds. Bruno M. Damiani and Ruth El Saffar. $30.00
51. *Discourse Studies in Honor of James L. Kinneavy*, ed. Rosalind J. Gabin. $45.00
52. John Guzzardo, *Textual History and the "Divine Comedy."* $40.50
53. Cheryl Brown Rush, *Circling Home*. Foreword by Sen. Eugene McCarthy. $24.50
54. Melinda Lehrer, *Classical Myth and the "Polifemo" of Góngora*. $39.50
55. Anne Thompson, *The Generation of '98: Intellectual Politicians*. $41.50
56. Salvatore Paterno, *The Liturgical Context of Early European Drama*. Preface by Lawrence Klibbe. $38.50
57. Maria Cecilia Ruiz, *Literatura y política: el "Libro de los estados" y el "libro de las armas" de Don Juan Manuel*. $37.50
58. James P. Gilroy, *Prévost's Mentors: The Master-Pupil Relationship in the Major Novels of the Abbé Prévost*. $39.95
59. *A Critical Edition of Juan Diamante's "La reina María Estuarda"* by Michael G. Paulson and Tamara Alvarez-Detrell. $44.50
60. David Craig, *Like Taxes: Marching Through Gaul*. Preface by Howard McCord. $21.50
61. M. Cecilia Colombi, *Los refranes en el "Quijote": texto y contexto*. Prólogo por Juan Bautista Avalle-Arce. $40.50
62. *"La mística ciudad de Dios"* (1670). *Edition and Study by* Augustine M. Esposito, O.S.A. $36.50
63. Salvatore Calomino, *From Verse to Prose: the Barlaam and Josaphat Legend in 15th Century Germany*. $50.00
64. Gene Fendt, *Works of Love? Reflection on Works of Love*. $37.50

BOOK ORDERS
* Clothbound. *All book orders*, except library orders, must be prepaid and addressed to **Scripta Humanística**, 1383 Kersey Lane, Potomac, Maryland 20854. *Manuscripts* to be considered for publication should be sent to the same address.

Like Taxes: Marching Through Gaul

Like Taxes:
Marching Through Gaul

David Craig

Scripta Humanistica

60

Craig, David, 1951-
   Like Taxes
      p. cm. — (Scripta Humanistica ; 60)
   ISBN 0-916379-67-5 : $21.50
      1. Christian   poetry,   American.   I. Titles.   II. Series: Scripta
Humanistica (Series) ; 60.
PS3553.R223L55   1989
   811'.54—dc20   89-10532
                                                                            CIP

                              Publisher and Distributor:
                              SCRIPTA HUMANISTICA
                                 1383 Kersey Lane
                           Potomac, Maryland, 20854, U.S.A.

                            © SCRIPTA HUMANISTICA
         Library of Congress Catalog Card Number   89-10532
                  International Standard Book Number   0-916379-65-5